Doing it for themselves: participation and black and minority ethnic service users

Nasa Begum

First published in Great Britain in July 2006
by the Social Care Institute for Excellence (SCIE) and the Race Equality Unit (REU)

© SCIE/REU 2006
All rights reserved

ISBN-10 1-904812 37-6
ISBN-13 978-1-904812-37-1

Written by Nasa Begum

Produced by The Policy Press
Fourth Floor, Beacon House
Queen's Road
Bristol BS8 1QU
tel 0117 331 4054
fax 0117 331 4093
tpp-info@bristol.ac.uk
www.policypress.org.uk

**This report is available online
www.scie.org.uk and www.reu.org.uk**

Social Care Institute for Excellence
Goldings House
2 Hay's Lane
London SE1 2HB
tel 020 7089 6840
fax 020 7089 6841
textphone 020 7089 6893
www.scie.org.uk

Race Equality Unit
Unit 35 Kings Exchange
Tileyard Road
London N7 9AH
tel 020 7619 6220
fax 020 7619 6230
www.reu.org.uk

Contents

Foreword	iv
Notes on the author	v
Summary	vii
Introduction	1
What is meant by participation	3
Approaches to participation	4
Participation and the social care landscape	5
Emergence of new social movements	6
Development of 'consumerist' and 'democratic' approaches	6
The move towards recognising diversity and difference	7
Diversity and equality	8
'Race' and equality and service user participation	9
Participation of black and minority ethnic service users: myths and realities	10
Favourable factors for enabling black and minority ethnic service user participation	16
Black and minority ethnic service user participation does work when properly supported	18
Social care 'professionals' working with black and minority ethnic service users as allies, advocates and brokers	19
Conclusion	20
References and note	23

Foreword

In November 2005 Nasa Begum delivered the Lord Pitt Memorial lecture on the subject 'is participation working for black and minority ethnic service users'? This paper, which is jointly published by SCIE and REU, is based on this lecture.

The Lord Pitt Memorial lecture is an annual event, established by REU, to mark the contribution made by Lord Pitt of Hampstead to promoting equality for Britain's black and minority ethnic communities. Lord Pitt became the first chair of REU, a national agency established in 1987 to: support the development of appropriate social care services to Britain's black and minority ethnic communities. He remained its chair until his death in 1994.

Lord Pitt was a widely respected campaigner for equality for Britain's black and minority ethnic communities, as well as being active within the medical profession and in politics, in particular the Labour Party. Within the medical profession he was one of the few black GP's of his time, and became the first and only black President of the British Medical Association, and in politics he made it to Parliament, when he was made Lord Pitt of Hampstead in 1975. However, his passion remained the fight against racial discrimination. He was intimately involved with a number of the campaigns and organisations promoting racial equality since the 1950s, with his surgery often used as a meeting place. He was one of the founders of the Anti-Apartheid Movement, and after a meeting with Dr Martin Luther King set up the 'Campaign Against Racial Discrimination' (CARD). It was pressure from CARD that led to the first piece of legislation outlawing racial discrimination and establishing Community Relations Commissions in 1968, which in 1976 came to be known as the Commission for Racial Equality.

In keeping with the tradition of fighting racial injustice and discrimination started by people like Lord Pitt, the Annual Lord Pitt Memorial lectures are delivered by leaders in the field of race equality and reflect on contemporary issues. In the spirit of that tradition, in this paper, an elaboration of the issues raised in her delivery of the Lord Pitt Memorial Lecture, Nasa Begum, an activist in the field of race and disability equality, opens up the challenge that will make the journey to black and minority ethnic service user participation happen.

Notes on the author

Nasa Begum has worked at SCIE as Principal Adviser Participation since 2003 with responsibility for ensuring that service user and carer participation is embedded throughout all of its work. Prior to this, as a qualified social worker, Nasa worked for local authority social services, King's Fund, Mind (National Association for Mental Health) and Policy Studies Institute in practitioner and policy/service development roles. She has a background in research and training and has published work on service user participation, race equality, gender, community care and independent living.

Nasa has used social care services throughout her life and been active in service user and carer participation work both in a professional and personal capacity for over 20 years.

Nasa has been on the board of many organisations ranging from an Asian women's resource centre, mental health system survivors organisation to a Black Disabled People's network and Greater London Association of Disabled people. She was Chair of Waltham Forest Association of Disabled People and the POWERHOUSE, an organisation of women with learning difficulties that set up the first ever refuge for women with learning difficulties.

In her 'spare' time Nasa is a board member of the National Centre for Independent Living and part of an 'experts by experience' group focusing on improving social care.

Dedicated to service users who are seldom heard, especially Haji Abdul Ghafar 1956-2005 (peace be upon him)

Summary

Service user participation in social care has increased markedly in the wider service user movement over the last 20 years, however, the participation of black and minority ethnic service users has diminished over the same period. This report identifies some of the reasons for this reduction, and concludes by stating that given the right opportunities, support and resources, there is genuine commitment and interest from service users to become more actively involved in the process.

Key points

- Over the last 20 years, mainstream service user participation in social care has increased markedly whereas black and minority ethnic participation has diminished over the same period.
- Policy-makers and practitioners often consult with black and minority ethnic professionals and community leaders, rather than going direct to service users themselves.
- There is no evidence to suggest that black and minority ethnic service users do not want to participate.
- Social care professionals have an important role to play in facilitating participation.
- Race equality issues must become part of mainstream activities.
- Black and minority ethnic service user participation does work when properly supported.

Participation: myths and realities

The Government's new white paper *Our health, our care, our say: a new direction for community services* states that people who use or require social care support are a fundamental resource in their own care and in determining the formulation of future policy and service developments. Despite a history of self-help and direct experience, black and minority ethnic service users (of all services) appear gradually to have become relatively passive. The reasons for this are varied and complex and many supposed explanations can be dispelled as prevailing myths that act as barriers to participation.

Policy-makers and practitioners often seek the participation of professionals and leaders within black and minority ethnic communities. They rarely attempt to engage black and minority ethnic service user themselves. There is ample evidence documenting the difficulties black and minority ethnic service users face in accessing and using services. It is also imperative for black and minority ethnic service users to be involved in the design, delivery and evaluation of services. Only then will they want to participate in the process.

Another myth states that participation is not a priority or as relevant to black and minority ethnic service users. Indeed, having difficulty accessing services may cause participation to be less of a priority unless it is at an individual level. Fear, lack of trust, and a feeling that one ought to appear forever grateful may also inhibit participation for some groups. But there is no evidence to suggest that black and minority ethnic service users do not want to participate at some level. Policy-makers need to keep an open mind and sometimes think laterally to facilitate the involvement of black and minority ethnic service users. They may need to be flexible and creative to do things differently to enable service users to participate in a way that is relevant and appropriate to them. They also need to reassure the service user that their involvement is more than merely consultative and can genuinely affect and shape policy.

Often when agencies want black and minority ethnic service users to participate, the first port of call is community 'leaders', voluntary sector workers and black and minority ethnic professionals. Indeed, they have been a loud voice in the struggle to put the needs of black and minority ethnic service users on the social care agenda. But a large proportion of these 'representatives' do not have direct experience of being social care service users. Possible solutions could include recruitment and appropriate training of black and minority ethnic staff. It is important though that they aren't forced into having to address race equality issues simply on the basis of their ethnic background.

Leading on from this, it must be acknowledged that the mainstream service user movement cannot represent black and minority ethnic service users until race equality and anti-discriminatory practice becomes integral to everyone's work. The service user movement is as likely to be as racist as any other part of society and for black and minority ethnic service users to feel less marginalised and to encourage greater participation, this must be addressed.

Social care professionals have an important role to play. They need to support the participation of service users to develop social care that promotes social inclusion, recognises service users as citizens and allocates services based on what service users define as important. The assumption that empowerment and participation requires social care professionals to take a back seat is short-sighted and naïve. They can be strong allies although the parameters of such partnerships must be agreed at the outset to ensure only the most appropriate pre-existing professional systems and structures are used.

Some positive signs

Black and minority ethnic service user participation can work when properly supported. One such success story is *Helping each other, helping ourselves*, a project run by Tasibee, an organisation that started out as a Pakistani Muslim women's prayer group. The project worked with Pakistani Muslim women with long-term mental health problems, who, through self-help groups and training, were able to become more assertive and confident.

Service Plus, which is run by the International Somali Community Trust, provides a range of services to Somali disabled people – many of whom are refugees or asylum seekers. A forum was created for disabled service users to enable them to voice their opinions. Much of the work centres on individual advocacy but the project is able to bring some of the genuine concerns raised in advocacy work to the service user forum for discussion.

Conclusion

Black and minority ethnic communities have a long history of self-help and direct experience. There are no reasons to suggest that participation cannot work for black and minority ethnic service users. If policy-makers and practitioners are to make a genuine commitment to developing social care services that are relevant, appropriate and based on the notions of choice, then it is imperative that black and minority ethnic service users are actively engaged. They need to be actively supported and their involvement must be real and constructive and not purely consultative.

Introduction

People in the 21st century expect services to be fast, high quality, responsive combined and fitted around their lives. All public services should put the person who uses them at their heart... There is solid evidence that care is less effective if people feel they are not in control. A fundamental aim is to make the actions and choices of people who use services the drivers of improvement.[1]

The government's white paper *Improving our health, our care, our say: A new direction for community services*[2] starts from the premise that people who use or require social care support are a fundamental resource in their own care and in determining the formulation of future policy and service developments. Service users[3] are regarded as active partners in providing a direction and contribution to the design and delivery of social care resources.

Since the early 1990s service user participation has been central to the reform of public services. It is now relatively unheard of to have policies or service delivery in social care without some reference to involving service users. This can happen in a myriad of ways with service users having varying levels of influence and decision-making powers. However, it is questionable whether a diverse range of service users have an opportunity to use their expertise and experience to drive improvements in social care and attain outcomes that are important and relevant to them.

Carr (2004), while reviewing the difference service user participation has made to social care, points out that 'attention to the diversity of service users in terms of race, culture, sexuality ... was lacking in mainstream services and participation initiatives. This relates to both diversity within user groups and the relative lack of knowledge about user participation for marginalised people. Service users who are marginalised from the mainstream can also be found to be under- or unrepresented in the participation intended to develop those services'.[4]

Fortunately, although the overall picture of black and minority ethnic service users' participation seems somewhat bleak we can take heart from projects where real inroads have been made. Shaping Our Lives National User Network (SOLNUN) worked with three different groups of black and minority ethnic service users in their project *Shaping Our Lives – From outset to outcome* (2003). One of the groups that was involved in this project was 'EDGE – Ethnic Disabled Group Emerged – a large group of black disabled people, which itself provides services and support to people'.[5] Another example of where black and minority ethnic service user participation has been successful is a project called ROOTS. Here a group of African Caribbean people with learning disabilities came together 'to use direct experience, shared learning and good practice examples to promote positive change in the attitudes of staff working for local service providers and the culture of other organisations'.[6]

This paper will argue that the journey to achieve black and minority ethnic service user participation is not made often enough and it is paved with twists and turns. Nevertheless, when time, energy and resources are invested in engaging and supporting black and minority ethnic service users, there are real opportunities for ensuring that social care resources are used effectively to achieve valued and meaningful outcomes.

To really get to grips with the participation of black and minority ethnic service users and what is happening, it is important to understand the key factors that have shaped the development of service user participation and how it is put into practice within a wider context. The first part of this paper focuses on what is meant by 'service user participation' and why it has become a foundation stone for developing policy and practice. This provides a useful backdrop to consider what has happened to black and minority ethnic service users' participation. There are lessons to be learnt by examining some of the myths and realities prevailing in this arena: it will be suggested that, on the whole, there is still a long way to go in facilitating meaningful and effective participation with a group of service users who are seldom heard and often marginalised.

As already mentioned, there are pockets of successful projects and initiatives in relation to black and minority ethnic service user participation, but 'pockets' is the defining feature. Many of these projects are under-resourced and overstretched with a short shelf life. For all those involved in service user participation, the challenge is to seize the moment. In whatever capacity one is involved in social care and wider social policy, action needs to be taken to ensure that the barriers to black and minority ethnic service user participation are tackled head on so that black and minority ethnic service users experience improved outcomes.

The central argument contained in this paper is that while, quite rightly, service user participation has moved on in leaps and bounds over the past 20 years, there has been a tendency to substitute the direct experience of black and minority ethnic service users with proxy representatives. Black and minority ethnic community 'leaders', voluntary sector workers and black and minority ethnic professionals have been seen as surrogate service users and been used as a conduit for service user participation. Without doubt they have played a valuable and vital role in meeting the needs of black and minority ethnic service users and plugged some major gaps in service provision where mainstream services were failing. Indeed, black and minority ethnic community 'leaders', voluntary sector workers and black and minority ethnic professionals have been a loud voice in the struggle to put the needs of black and minority ethnic service users on the social care agenda.

The concepts of citizenship, social inclusion, consumerism, empowerment among others have become the bedrock of public policy and the reform of social 'welfare'. Therefore, there is no substitute for the real lived experience and insight of being a black and minority ethnic person who requires or uses social care resources. Those who work around or represent black and minority ethnic perspectives without direct experience of using social care have a critical part to play in supporting and facilitating the participation of black and minority ethnic service users, but cannot be their authoritative voice.

If policy makers and practitioners are to make a genuine commitment to developing social care services that are relevant, appropriate and based on the notions of choice, control, self-determination, autonomy, independence, social inclusion, citizenship and improving service outcomes for all service users then it is absolutely imperative that black and minority ethnic service users are actively engaged with policy and service development so that, in the words of singer/songwriter Annie Lennox, black and minority ethnic service users, are 'doing it for themselves'.

It is important to acknowledge that although the focus here is on black and minority ethnic service users, this does not mean that the perspectives and contributions of black and minority ethnic carers are not important or significant. Indeed, many of the issues raised are also relevant to the participation of carers. However, the experiences of carers are often different (but not unrelated) to that of service users. Black and minority ethnic carers, as the people who provide essential support and plug many of the gaps in social care, offer a valuable insight and perspective. Therefore, the contribution of black and minority ethnic carers needs to be debated, analysed and articulated by a carer who has direct personal experience of providing what is commonly known as 'informal care'. Meanwhile, this paper will take the view that carers who require social care support themselves need to be treated as service users in their own right.

What is meant by participation?

'Participation' and 'user involvement' have become common currency. The two terms are somewhat imprecise and used interchangeably. Reaching a consensus about the distinction between participation and user involvement is difficult. For the sake of simplicity user involvement can be regarded as a component of participation.

User involvement has been defined as 'participation of users of services in decisions that affect their lives (at an individual level)'.[7] Collectively involvement can include participation in decision making, policy formulation, service development and in the running and controlling of services.

Based on the practice guide *Participation of children and young people in developing social care*[8], this paper defines participation as:

- ... involvement in individual decisions about their own lives, as well as collective involvement in matters which affect them
- a culture of listening which enables (service users) to influence both decisions about the services they receive as individuals on a day-to-day basis, as well as how those services are developed and delivered for all (service users) who access them
- not an isolated activity, but a process by which (service users) are empowered and supported to influence change either within an organisation or by directly leading in policy and service development
- not a hierarchy (as Arnstein[9] suggests in the ladder of involvement) where the aim is to reach the top of the ladder ... different levels of participation are valid for different groups of (service users) and at different stages of policy and service development.

While different groups may define participation in different ways, in general there is widespread agreement at a national and local level that participation is important and worthwhile.

Approaches to participation

Participation can be perceived as a journey to improve outcomes for service users, but instead of professionals being in the driving seat, service users and professionals travel together. The routes available to initiate and promote participation can range from consultation activities and service user-led research to service users directly working with their constituencies to develop policies and provide services (that is, advocacy and direct payments support) through service user-controlled organisations.

Wright et al (2006) point out that effective service user participation requires agencies to adopt a whole systems approach that focuses on four interacting elements:

> Culture: the ethos of an organisation, shared by staff and service users, which demonstrates a commitment to participation.
> Structure: the planning, development and resourcing of participation evident in an organisation's infrastructures.
> Practice: the ways of working, methods for involvement, skills and knowledge which enable ... [service users] to become involved.
> Review: the monitoring and evaluation systems which enable an organisation to evidence change affected by ... participation.[10]

By adopting a 'whole systems' approach it is possible to embed participation into the fabric of health and social care. Nevertheless, it is prudent to remember *why* a particular journey is being made and *where* the final destination needs to be. The goal of participation must be to initiate and sustain change and improvement so that health and social care resources are used effectively to improve outcomes for service users.

Robson et al (2003) draws a distinction between management-centred user involvement and user-centred user involvement. The former involves service users working within existing structures and the agenda being defined by the agency concerned. 'The organisations experience less actual change or pressure to change but their profile and reputation is enhanced.'[11] User-centred user involvement 'meant that service users were able to pursue their own objectives and priorities and had opportunities to organise and meet in ways that suited them. This kind of involvement led to benefits for service users as individuals and their groups'.[12]

In social care there has been a combination of management-centred user involvement and user-centred user involvement, the latter being particularly relevant to the philosophy and method of working employed within service user-controlled organisations. Statutory, private and voluntary sector service providers are more likely to accommodate service users within established systems and draw on a management-centred user involvement approach. However, often a mixture of approaches will be employed depending on the context and circumstances in which user involvement is being applied.

Regardless of the approach or methods used to facilitate service user participation there can be little doubt that considerable effort and resources have been invested. Less attention has been paid to what impact or affect service user participation has had on the development and delivery of social care services. Carr (2004) points out 'there is some knowledge about participation techniques but little or no examination of the relationship between the process and the achievement of tangible user-led change. This is not to say that certain participation initiatives are not contributing to the improvement of services for the people who use them, but that those changes are not being monitored and evaluated'.[13]

Participation has to be seen as a means to an end rather than an end in itself. There is a danger that service user participation can become another process to be completed and rendered a 'tick box' exercise, rather than being recognised as an essential tool for improving social care. Fundamentally, service user participation is a vehicle for making sure agencies are using the right mode of transport and relevant map to reach the desired final destination – effective outcomes for service users.

To understand how and why service user participation has become a central feature of the social care landscape it is worth taking a step backwards to identify some of the dynamics that have led to where social care policy and practice is today.

Participation and the social care landscape

There have been a number of different influences (often interrelated) that have positioned service user participation at the heart of social care policy and practice, which are elaborated on below.

- **Re-kindling of interest in human rights.** For a long time different groups within the service user movement have argued that public services such as social care should be rooted in a rights-based framework. One of the criticisms of the NHS Community Care Act 1990 and subsequent legislation and guidance has been the emphasis on a needs-led rather than a rights-based approach. A needs-led framework invests a great deal in practitioners making judgements about what a person's needs are and whether social care resources can be allocated. The Human Rights Act 1998 represented a significant advancement in the development of a human rights framework which enables service users to challenge organisational and professional decisions that may infringe on their human rights.
- **Re-emergence of the idea of citizenship.** Since the early 1980s service users have fought a long and hard campaign in demanding civil rights. Imperative to the call for civil rights was the belief that disabled people and mental health system survivors should be recognised as citizens who should play an integral role in developing services. The phrase 'nothing about us without us' coined by the disability movement reflected the fact that disabled people were not prepared to be passive recipients of care. Instead they pushed to be treated as active partners in determining and delivering the resources required to enable them to live as full members of society. The notion of citizenship and service users having a direct say over the issues that affect their lives underpinned the growth and interest in service user participation.

Parallel to service users advocating and demanding their rights as citizens, New Labour under the Blair government has invested a lot of energy in encouraging the idea of participatory rights of citizens, twinned with a philosophy of individual and collective responsibility.

Citizenship, rights and responsibilities are the bedrock of much public sector reform. This is evident in the abundance of initiatives, at both central and local government level, giving people the right of decision making and a role in influencing policy and service development. This can be witnessed through policies and practices promoting 'parent power' in schools, patients' forums, the publication of league tables, Best Value reviews and a raft of projects designed to involve local communities in the regeneration of their neighbourhoods.

The growing expectation of individual responsibility combined with a philosophy of self-reliance has permeated social care at a macro and micro level. As a consequence, there has been a gradual shift in thinking: instead of professionals knowing best, service users are now expected to be part of the process of finding solutions.

The green paper (2005) *Youth matters*[14] establishes a strategic direction with numerous proposals giving young people the right to access a range of activities and opportunities. However, these come at a price with penalties for anti-social behaviour or failure to fulfil one's responsibilities. Exercising personal responsibility has been at the heart of the discourse surrounding the reform of young people's services.

Emergence of new social movements

The main thrust for change in user involvement came from the disability movement and mental health system survivors. These movements organised themselves on the basis of a shared experience of discrimination and dissatisfaction with service provision. Recognising that the personal is political they lobbied, campaigned and initiated change and improvements by developing services that helped achieve the outcomes that disabled people and mental health system survivors wanted. Initiatives such as direct payments, independent living, peer and self-advocacy, self-help and user-controlled networks all emerged from the leadership, creativity and persistence generated within the service user movement.

Development of 'consumerist' and 'democratic' approaches

Participation, it can be argued, broadly falls into two main philosophies. The first is the 'consumerist' approach where service users are regarded as consumers whose choice and requirements can influence services in the market place. This is underpinned by the idea that if service users' requirements are identified then service providers can offer more efficient and economic services. Beresford (2001) argues that a distinction is created between citizens/public and the 'otherness' of welfare users. He writes that this otherness '... is epitomised by the New Right's conceptualisation of *welfare users* as wealth *consuming*, and a cost to *public/citizens*, who are contrasted as wealth *creating*'.[15]

From the 1980s to the present, a commitment to market forces and consumerism has encouraged statutory health and social services agencies to contract out the direct provision of services to private and voluntary organisations. Often referred to as the 'contract culture', this enabled voluntary organisations to bid to provide services, which they have done (partly at least) on the grounds of their responsiveness to, and involvement of, service users.

The second approach is the democratic one, where the 'primary concern has been with empowerment, the redistribution of power, and people gaining more control over their lives. The concern is with how we are treated and supported to live as equal citizens so that we can achieve our civil rights and equality of opportunity'.[16]

The consumerist approach focuses on organisational needs (such as managing budgets) and working with service providers to meet professionally-assessed needs. On the other hand, the democratic approach emerges from service users' rights and requirements, and it is based on the experience and perspectives of service users and their organisations.[17]

Interestingly, the white paper *Our health, our care, our say: A new direction for community services* (2006),[18] appears to straddle the two approaches with both consumerist and democratic components. For example, the endorsement of the idea of self-assessment starts from the premise that service users (with support if necessary) can define their own requirements, then possibly go on to control an individual budget and/or direct payment. The fact that service providers will have to develop their services in accordance with what service users are looking to purchase, and respond to the needs identified by those who may have third parties representing them, suggests that a consumerist model will remain in force.

The move towards recognising diversity and difference

This approach encapsulates a multitude of issues and shifts in thinking. Perhaps the most important one to acknowledge is that service users are not a homogeneous group. Many factors will have an affect on the type and level of participation in which service users engage: age, sexuality, type of impairment, immigration status, legal status in terms of offending behaviour, being a looked after child, detention under the Mental Health Act 1983 or having a child(ren) on the child protection register. For example, a parent might be involved in a family group conference or discussions at a child protection case review, but the degree of influence and decisions they can make will be much more limited than those of a young person involved in designing a life skills course for teenage mothers.

There are significant disparities between the levels and kind of participation working-age adults are involved with, and the levels to which children, young people or even older people are involved. Going back to the green paper *Youth matters*[19] there is a strong emphasis on the involvement of young people in policy and service development. Nevertheless, on closer scrutiny the involvement advocated is predominately in the form of consultation, rather than using a range of participatory approaches. That is, to share power and control in the design, delivery and evaluation of policies and services which matter to young people.

Some of the differences in the participation of different groups within the service user constituency is influenced by issues of capacity, expectations or a culture of not having a sufficient range of resources, techniques and approaches available to be used readily and with confidence. There is an established history of participation initiatives focusing on the more visible, organised and vocal groups of service users. Equally, it is probably fair to say that social care agencies have not, until relatively recently, recognised and started to address the fact that some service user constituencies have been left out in the cold in relation to participation activities.

Carr's (2004) review of service user participation points out: '... attention to the diversity of service users in terms of race, culture, sexuality ... was lacking in mainstream services and participation initiatives... Living in rural or certain geographical areas can have a bearing on exclusion from structures for participation. The very young and the very old (particularly those with dementia), the homeless and travellers, people in institutional or residential care, people with addiction problems and those with severe disabilities and high support needs ... seldom have the opportunity to be heard or to influence service change'.[20]

The tendency within social care to date has been to label those service users who are excluded or marginalised from services or participation processes as 'hard to reach'. This implies that the problems are associated with the individuals, rather than recognising and responding to the fact that the difficulties lie with agencies who find certain groups of service users harder to reach or engage with.

Referring specifically to hearing the voices of and engaging with black and minority ethnic service users, Carr (2004) explains that they '... may have difficulty in subordinating their objectives to the narrow [services] agenda, and may be unwilling to act as collaborators ... it [has been] argued that for some people previous attempts to influence health and social care services have proved unsatisfactory'.[21]

Diversity and equality

To understand why the participation of black and minority ethnic service users might seem unsatisfactory, it is important to place it in the context of broader diversity and equality debates.

Diversity has become common currency in public discourse over the past few years especially in the wake of the Macpherson report into the death of Stephen Lawrence. Butt (2006) defines diversity to mean 'taking account of the complexities of the lives of individuals and of groups of people, and the impact of these complexities on their experience of discrimination and disadvantage.'[22] Such a definition avoids seeing service users in relation to single equality groups, according to their gender, 'race', disability, age, sexuality, religion and faith or social class and so on. The strength of this definition rests with the fact that simultaneous or compound discrimination and oppression can easily be accommodated and addressed. Nevertheless, critics argue that by promulgating the idea that all types of differences and inequalities come under one roof, there is a danger that it waters down or diverts attention from the specifics of the distinct types of inequalities and what is required to tackle them. Moreover, the term 'diversity' (although often used interchangeably with 'race' equality) fails to convey what has to be challenged and what needs to be achieved in the way that 'anti-racism', 'multi-culturalism', 'race equality' among others make explicit.

The shift away from naming the specifics of the different inequalities people encounter to a more integral and diversity-based stance is reflected in the government's move to establish a Commission for Single Equality and Human Rights Commission (CEHR).[23] It remains to be seen how effectively CEHR will rise to the challenge of subsuming the work of the current Equal Opportunities Commission, Disability Rights Commission and Commission for Racial Equality, while due regard is given to the explicit situations and experiences encountered by various groups of people.

Changes in the approach taken to addressing equality and diversity combined with significant transformations taking place in the way social care resources are designed and delivered, means that now is an opportune moment to explore the participation of black and minority ethnic service users.

'Race' equality and service user participation

When looking at the participation of service users who are diverse because of their ethnic, religious, cultural or linguistic background and immigration status, it is evident that much less progress has been made in this area than in the wider sphere of user participation. The reasons for this are varied and complex and are discussed in more depth later. Yet it is probably not unreasonable to say that policy makers, commissioners and providers have focused their attention primarily on service user groups that are more vocal, active and organised, or where supporting a group's engagement has been relatively straightforward providing the time and resources are invested. Equally, for a host of possibly similar or different reasons within service user groups and organisations (particularly the lack of voluntary sector capacity building), the participation of black and minority ethnic service users has often, at best, been an afterthought or marginalised and sometimes excluded altogether. The same criticism has been levelled at black and minority ethnic organisations who, while being very active in campaigning, advocacy work and service provision, have shown a limited, and sometimes absent, commitment and ability to actively promote the involvement of their service users.

Evans and Banton (2001) write that 'attitudes towards 'race' within white organisations and disability within black organisations have created major barriers to the involvement of black disabled people'.[24] This argument may seem very appealing, but it is somewhat simplistic. Although many disabled people may also be service users (and carers), social care service users are drawn from a much wider section of society. For example, non-disabled children and families constitute one of the largest groups of service users in social care. Yet the participation of black and minority ethnic children and families in social care is limited. The REU (formerly the Race Equality Unit) programme 'Strengthening Families, Strengthening Communities' [25] has played an important role in enabling black and minority ethnic parents to take much more control of their lives. There can be little doubt that taking control (with support if necessary) is an essential component of participation. Further work is required to identify methods that focus on the involvement of black and minority ethnic children and young people, both as individuals in their own right and as part of families and communities.

From the knowledge that exists about service user participation it is clear that there are a variety of ways to promote user involvement. These need to be adapted and used according to the context, task in hand and the group(s) of service users being engaged with. This can range from involvement in assessments and/or case reviews, to being part of a user-controlled organisation providing advocacy and a direct payments service. There is no reason to suggest that black and minority ethnic service users do not value what participation has to offer. A group of African-Caribbean people with learning disabilities express, very poignantly, the importance and role of self-advocacy in their lives. 'Making sure people listen to you and know what you want is very important for people who have little power and are likely to be treated unfairly. There are lots of different ways of getting your views and interests across to workers and professionals in care services but speaking for yourself is by far the best... Self-advocacy helps all people to know what they want and be stronger in standing up for their rights.'[26]

Undoubtedly, black and minority ethnic service users have a lot to say about and to contribute to social care. This energy and potential has to be realised through ensuring resources and a range of participatory techniques are employed to facilitate black and minority ethnic service users' participation. However, if the participation of black and minority ethnic service users was just simply (putting it at its crudest) a matter of providing a bit of funding or having interpreters available at a focus group meeting, then it is more than likely that social care would be much further behind than is currently the case.

To move forward, it is necessary to look backward and explore the myths and realities that prevail and militate against service user participation within black and minority ethnic communities. Some of these myths will be addressed below. Then we will examine some of the factors that indicate a promising future for black and minority ethnic service user participation.

Participation of black and minority ethnic service users: myths and realities

Myth: 'We don't know what black and minority ethnic service users want' or 'they look after their own'.

Reality: there is a plethora of research and literature spanning a period of over 16 years which documents the difficulties of black and minority ethnic service users accessing and using services. In 1990, Begum wrote in a research project on the lives of Asian disabled people and carers in Waltham Forest that 'the take up of services was very low. Lack of information, linguistic barriers, racism, religious and cultural insensitivity were just some of the reasons why people did not use services or stopped using them'.[27] Five years later in *Beyond samosas and reggae* Begum raised the same concerns again: 'The take-up of services ... appears to be very low. Yet, there is no evidence to suggest that black disabled people do not need or wish to use services... Securing essential services can be like an obstacle course that has to be carefully negotiated. Lack of communication, poor access to information and inappropriate assessment procedures and service provision have all been identified as additional barriers that prevent black disabled people from taking up services'.[28]

In 2004, the Joseph Rowntree Foundation produced a report summarising its work on ethnicity. The findings suggest that stereotypes and assumption, prejudice and discrimination, mono-cultural service provision and lack of information are major barriers.[29] In *Breaking the circles of fear: A review of the relationship between mental health services and African and Caribbean communities* (2004), the Sainsbury Centre for Mental Health argue that 'stereotypical views of black people, racism, cultural ignorance and the stigma and anxiety associated with mental illness often combine to undermine the way in which mental health services assess and respond to the needs of African Caribbean communities'.[30]

Black and minority ethnic service users have repeatedly talked about the barriers faced when trying to access or use services. There is ample evidence to point policy makers and practitioners in the right direction. However, the myth about not knowing what black and minority ethnic people need, or the belief that 'they' don't want the services provided and look after their own remains ubiquitous.

Begum declared in 2002 '... one would be forgiven for thinking that by now agencies would have been able to move forward and improve provision significantly. It is somewhat worrying that, more often than not, we still find ourselves ... being called upon to explain what the issues are for us and what we need from services ... the current emphasis on user involvement should offer a framework for involving us, in the design, delivery and evaluation of services rather than just consulting us as part of some research'.[31]

Myth: Participation is not a priority or as relevant to black and minority ethnic service users.

Reality: There can be little doubt that for any service user a struggle to access or use services may mean that participation is not a priority unless it is at an individual level to improve their personal circumstances and get out of crisis situations. The experience of many black and minority ethnic service users can be so negative in relation to accessing social care that there may be a reluctance to participate at any level, whether individual or more strategic. However, this does not mean that the opportunities to participate are not revisited or reviewed as circumstances and experiences change.

Ibrahim (2003), talking about the participation of Asian women mental health service users, explains: 'There needs to be a balance so that when a woman is experiencing difficulties most with managing her mental distress, that is not the point at which she is asked to sit on a community group's (or other) committee where she is a token user. We need to remember the old saying that when someone complains of a hole in their roof they should not be told to join a tenants group. Joining the tenants group may well be an option for the future; the individual's potential to contribute must not be underestimated, but first things first: what they need right now is some help to mend the roof'.[32]

Another major issue for some groups of black and minority ethnic service users is the whole area of trust, fear of repercussions and an inclination to feel that one ought to appear forever grateful. Refugees and asylum seekers who use or require social care are particularly affected by these issues. The great effort required to have very basic human needs met means that for some refugees and asylum seekers the daily battle becomes all too much. As one asylum seeker explains, 'I am depressed most of the time. I feel like running away because it seems nobody listens to me or give me even small money for transport. I appear to be rude to people because I am depressed and I am constantly asking for the basics'.[33] Another asylum seeker talks about the difficult situation asylum seekers are faced with: '... when you are in someone's country you are a beggar despite the circumstances you were fleeing from your own country. Also if you had a better life before you feel humiliated here by the way you are treated. Less than human. You are constantly begging, you either get or you don't, then you do not bother anymore'.[34]

For many refugees and asylum seekers the suggestion of participating in how services should be designed and delivered, or even expressing a personal opinion about whether something is good or bad is a complete flight of fantasy. The overwhelming fear of the minimal support they receive being withdrawn is so real that saying anything else is out of the question. One refugee who took part in the consultation on the Green Paper *Independence, well being and choice: Vision for adult social care in England*[35] was so worried about participating she said, 'Please do not mention my name... I am a refugee in this country and my right is not the same as British people. There's bad news about refugees and asylum seekers in the UK. So if you say something maybe they will think I am not thankful to them, I mean social services and the Refugee Council'.[36]

Myth: They (black and minority ethnic service users) are not interested in participation.

Reality: With the proviso that the timing of participation and service users' personal circumstances are carefully balanced, there is no evidence to suggest that black and minority ethnic service users do not want to participate at some level. Ibrahim (2003) complains, 'I constantly hear how Asian women (service) users/survivors 'do not want to be involved, are not interested, are apathetic, demotivated', the list goes on. Where is the user-led research to back this?'.[37]

In 1995 Begum wrote that black and minority ethnic service users '... should be involved in the development of services, but there are only a handful of black user groups. Through self-help people are able to develop their self-confidence, consider different options and prepare a collective response, reflecting a diverse range of needs'.[38]

Butt and O'Neil (2004) in *Let's move on: Black and minority ethnic older people's views on research findings*, report that '... there are many different possible designs for involvement, but there is a single strong message that came through. Black older people had frequently been consulted but seldom involved in the shaping of research or development work. The standards of involvement that the groups implied were about:

- Being involved right from the start of initiatives.
- Having more than just one or two token members on a group.
- Having a real say in decisions about the initiative.
- Meeting regularly and having regular updates on progress.
- Being supported in the process and not simply left with a series of inaccessible papers to read.
- Being given the results of research – not simply being the subjects whose knowledge is taken.
- Having a say in the meaning of the results and how these will be used'.[39]

These are not new messages – throughout the work of the service user movement and the host of participation projects that have been instigated, the same messages have emerged. Nevertheless, stereotypes and perceptions of black and minority ethnic older people (not understanding, being unable to communicate or not wanting to be involved) do not easily fit with the idea of them taking an active participatory role in the design, fieldwork and analysis of research.

Ibrahim argues '... the user involvement agenda is as valid and important to Asian women service users and survivors as any other group. This does not mean we are only called upon to supply quotes for annual reports, inform research studies, complete evaluation exercises, provide personal 'case' studies ... our knowledge and expertise must be used throughout the planning, implementation and evaluation processes to promote choice, empowerment, self determination (and participation) ... the question is whether services are ready to share power and control, or whether (we) will always be relegated to a position where others expect to save us and show us the light'.

Black and minority ethnic service users are caught in a real dilemma. They may be keen to participate and be involved but repeated consultation exercises with no feedback or evidence of change leads to 'consultation fatigue'. Trivedi (2002) explains: 'Others (service users) would like to work for change but are cynical and doubt (our) voices will ever be heard or (our) views taken on board and (our) issues meaningfully addressed. Others may be more optimistic but may instinctively know or have learned from experience that working within established user system would be inappropriate for (us)'.[40]

People need to keep an open mind and sometimes think laterally to facilitate the participation of black and minority ethnic service users. Sometimes traditional participation methods of meetings, debates, focus groups and so on may be appropriate. At other times, there needs to be flexibility and creativity to do things differently so that service users can participate in a way that is relevant, appropriate and meaningful to them.

Members of Share in Maudsley Black Action (SIMBA), a black and minority ethnic user/survivor group at the Maudsley Hospital in south London, explain: '... we were quite clear we did not want the traditional user involvement model of meetings, committees and paperwork. We knew we had to use other ways of getting our message across... We decided we would use art, music, poetry and writing to raise our issues and campaign for change, enabling as many people as wanted to become involved'.[41]

Myth: 'We (social care agencies) work with community 'leaders', black and minority ethnic voluntary sector organisations and black and minority ethnic professionals in our workforce'.

Reality: Often when agencies want black and minority ethnic service users to participate, the first port of call is community 'leaders', voluntary sector groups and black and minority ethnic staff that they employ. This puts a huge responsibility on the shoulders of these professionals in what can be very demanding circumstances.

No suggestion is being made that community 'leaders', voluntary sector organisations and black and minority ethnic staff do not have the skills and knowledge to advocate and represent black and minority ethnic service users. Indeed, many have done excellent work in what are, often, very difficult situations. Nevertheless, the elephant in the room that is not being discussed and debated is the fact that a large proportion of these 'representatives' do not have direct experience of being social care service users. They are not immune from being prejudiced, discriminating and holding stereotypical views of service users and what 'they' need. Therefore, encouraging the participation of black and minority ethnic people who do not or have not used social care services might provide a short cut or seem an obvious solution to the participation of service users, but participation through surrogates can never be an acceptable or plausible alternative to black and minority ethnic service user participation. Begum (2002) points out that '... it is important to remember that non-disabled (or those who have not used services) have a valuable and significant role to play in terms of accessing people and taking on an advocacy role, but this is not a substitute for user involvement'.[42]

Lessons need to be learnt from domestic violence, child protection, forced marriages and 'ritualistic' abuse work within black and minority ethnic communities, where working in partnership with community 'leaders' and some of the obvious representatives in black and minority ethnic communities did not lead to a discovery of what was really happening on the ground. For example, child abuse and domestic violence are real taboo issues and remained undisclosed because community 'leaders' were not willing and/or able to deal with them. It was only when people who were living with the reality of these problems used their voices to speak out about the affects on their lives and the services they required to stay safe and be supported that things began to change. Proxy participation is unlikely to yield an adequate understanding of black and minority ethnic service users' lives and what interventions (if any) are needed to ensure their safety, respect and dignity and to promote choice and independence.

The solution for improving services is often said to be the recruitment and training of black and minority ethnic staff, and there can be little doubt that this would help greatly. Repeatedly service users have reported the need for black and minority ethnic staff and better training. However, we need to err on the side of caution, as there are two salient points to be made. The first is that black and minority ethnic staff should not be pigeon-holed into addressing 'race' equality issues if they do not wish to: they should have access to the same range of career development opportunities as others. Equally, given all workers have a responsibility to promote 'race' equality and anti-discriminatory practice, action must be taken to ensure it is integral to *everyone's* work. The second point is that through the use of training, supervision, workload management and other resources black and minority ethnic staff must be equipped to, and supported in, fulfilling their roles effectively, whether they work in 'specialist' diversity jobs, or are part of wider mainstream work. Likewise, the mechanisms of supervision, training, workload management, appraisals and other resources should be used to enable the wider social care workforce to deliver on its responsibility to promote 'race' equality and anti-discriminatory practice.

Begum (2002) reminds us that '… recruiting and training black people are often heralded as the essential ingredients for improving services. But if policies and working practices do not change and an environment is not created where there is a real willingness to respond sensitively and appropriately such initiatives will make no noticeable difference'.[43]

Myth: Service user (and survivor) movement embraces and represents black and minority ethnic service users.

Reality: The concerns raised about black and minority ethnic organisations addressing participation in many ways are reflected conversely when considering how service user organisations and the wider disability movement have included black and minority ethnic service users.

A mainstream user-controlled organisation remarked that '… it is not surprising that there has been much discussion about user involvement and participation. There has, however, been a noticeable lack of involvement by black disabled people..'.[44]

The reality is that the service user movement is as likely to be as racist as any other part of society. Therefore representing and/or involving black and minority ethnic service users has not always been integral (and sometimes completely excluded) in the participation work they have undertaken. However, it is important to acknowledge that the service user movement is no more and no less likely to be racist.

A Sainsbury Centre for Mental Health report (2003) *On our own terms*[45] found that black people were marginalised within the service user movement. It recommended the development of a national voice for the black and minority ethnic service user movement. Similarly *Breaking the circles of fear*[46] recommended that the Sainsbury Centre for Mental Health facilitate the development of a national voice for the black and minority ethnic service user movement. Two years after these recommendations were made there appears to be little activity to suggest a national service user led voice has been established, nor is there information in the public (service user movement) domain about progress or obstacles to the establishment of a national black and minority ethnic service user voice. Some progress has been made with small groups of black and minority ethnic service users coming together. These tend to be management centered user involvement rather than something driven and owned by service users.

Fortunately, some service user-controlled organisations have undertaken targeted specific work to facilitate the participation of black and minority ethnic service users. For example, Shaping Our Lives National User Network's project called *Shaping Our lives – From outset to outcome* worked with a group run by black and minority ethnic disabled people and two groups run by black mental health service users to evaluate what people think of the social care services they use. As a result of engaging with black mental health service users, the project concluded that the following was crucial to social care outcomes: '… the relationship between professionals and [service] users needs to be improved. Members of the group felt that they were not respected and were even ignored, and they wanted improvements in consultations with them. They felt that the black voice was unheard … there was quite a lot of pessimism about how, when and why? things would change … users did not want to do anything out of the ordinary and yet they were not able to do what they wanted … people did not feel comfortable going to social services to arrange this…'.[47]

The service user movement and the wider disability movement have done substantial work to demand that traditional voluntary organisations become more user-centred and ideally work towards becoming user-controlled. Many of the large national charities have now recognised the importance of user involvement, even if the concept of being user-controlled may seem a step to far. Consequently, a variety of participatory approaches have been adopted, from recruiting service users to senior management positions, to changing membership and governance arrangements. The visibility and presence of black and minority ethnic service users in the major national charities tends to remains low, though some have race or diversity specific posts, this has not been translated into supporting black and minority ethnic service users to have greater active involvement in the planning and decision making process. If the wider service user movement, in their campaigning and other work, ensured that the participation of black and minority ethnic service users was integral to everything they did, then rightly or wrongly the large national organisations might begin to take notice.

Work with black and minority ethnic service users should not be restricted to specific projects – these can be very valuable, but service user participation also needs to be part of the mainstream service user movement agenda.

Favourable factors for enabling black and minority ethnic service user participation

Strong history of self-help and direct action by black and minority ethnic communities

The history of black and minority ethnic people is rich in ground-breaking direct action and self-help. This played a central role in creating community cohesion, and in providing direction on how issues faced by black and minority ethnic communities should be dealt with. The fact that people had direct experience of racism, poverty, poor working conditions and social exclusion meant that they used a common shared experience to campaign, lobby, develop resources and inform policy. The language used might have focused on self-help, community action and community development, yet the principles of participation, that of people with direct experience getting involved and leading initiatives was very much at the heart of what was happening.

Despite a history of self-help and direct experience it is surprising to find that black and minority ethnic service users (of whatever type of service) appear to have gradually become relatively passive. Workers and management committee members who do not have direct experience of being service users have taken the lead and gradually pushed black and minority ethnic service users to the margins or excluded them altogether.

In defence of black and minority ethnic community organisations, it has been argued that so much time, energy and resources have to be put in to challenging and combating racism that stigma, discrimination, disempowerment and oppression faced by service users cannot be tackled or becomes a low priority. There has to come a point (hopefully very soon) when community groups and services can no longer justify a lack of action around service user involvement at a variety of levels. Arguments that black and minority ethnic community organisations and services are too busy tackling racism do not hold water. Participation has to be at the forefront of shaping the design and delivery of campaigns, policy development and services.

It is difficult to know to what extent the 'contract culture', time-limited funding, lack of resource management and organisational development or a de-politicisation of self-help and community action has led to a colonisation of community-led services by workers and management committees that do not have direct experience of being a service user (of whatever kind). Ibrahim (2003) writes '... the workers take on the role of being the 'professionals' and little attention is paid to ensuring that the more problematic practices found in mainstream services that disempower and alienate ... users and survivors are not perpetuated'.[48]

And there are signs, particularly in the mental health sector, that organisations are slowly waking up to the fact service users should have an active role developing and delivering services rather than passive recipients of welfare.

Morris (1999) talks about how Jewish Care has worked to tackle discrimination and provide services but, in the process, sometimes excluded service users in the way services are provided. 'We have always prided ourselves in being able to 'look after our own'. However, there is a downside, and that is that we provide care in a very paternalistic way, our systems tending to be patriarchal and hierarchical, and the services given in a benevolent manner, with issues like user involvement, until very recently, trailing a long way behind.'[49]

Ibrahim (2003) argues, 'It is now time to build on the knowledge and expertise acquired through grassroots work on domestic violence, immigration, racism, poor working conditions and so on. The direct experience of (those) who have encountered hostility and oppression in these areas has been fundamental to shaping developments and service responses'.[50] One has to remember how in the 1970s' Grunswick strike, and 30 years later the Gate Gourmet strike, it was primarily Asian women who took action against poor pay and working conditions. Similarly, domestic violence projects and services were very much set up, managed and delivered by women who had experienced domestic violence. These days such services would be described as 'user-controlled' because they are provided and managed by women with direct experience of domestic violence.

Valuable lessons should be learnt from the words of Kuyek and Labonte (1995) when they write: 'Our history is full of stories of the oppressed rebelling against the rebellor, only to reinstate an equally oppressive system. What we learn from oppression is how to oppress. If we want truly transformative politics then we must take up methods of social change – methods of empowerment..'.[51]

Black and minority ethnic service user participation does work when properly supported

There can be no getting away from the fact that black and minority ethnic service user participation requires proper resources, practical support, time, energy and commitment. Nevertheless, some examples have already been cited where participation has worked very well. Although a lack of secure funding, being over-stretched, lack of capacity building and organisational development, and a shortage of paid workers are all issues for black and minority ethnic service users, there is a real glimmer of hope with a mixture of projects springing up with black and minority ethnic service user participation at the core of their development.

Some organisations have used techniques such as providing benefits advice, language and sewing classes or a social group to encourage black and minority ethnic service users to come through the door on a regular basis. Such forums offer a sense of safety, which, in turn, often leads to other participation activities.

A good practice-based example of how participation has been nurtured is a project called *Helping each other, helping ourselves* run by Tasibee, an organisation that started out as a Pakistani Muslim prayer group. It was set up 'to promote participation a number of Pakistani Muslim women with long term mental health problems were trained to develop their confidence and skills through coming together in self-help groups, using life-story work as a vehicle for empowerment and change. Two further self-help groups were run, one for older women and one for young mothers, helping women to build on their strengths and become more assertive and confident.'[52]

Service Plus, run by International Somali Community Trust (ISCOM), provides a range of services to disabled Somali people (many of whom are refugees and asylum seekers). To bring about change through empowering service users to voice their opinions, a forum was created for disabled service users. Much of the work concentrated on individual advocacy, but the project worker was able to bring some of the genuine concerns raised in the advocacy work to the service user forum for discussion.[53]

Black and minority ethnic service users have formed user-controlled forums and organisations so that they can take the lead and shape the nature of their own participation. Equalities National,[54] an organisation for black and minority ethnic disabled people and carers, not only directly provides services but also contributes to policy and service development at different levels. Similarly, Asian People with Disabilities Alliance[55] and Awaaz[56] are all examples of service users coming together to share experiences and work on improving services.

Social care 'professionals' working with black and minority ethnic service users as allies, advocates and brokers

As has already been said, participation can be in many guises and at a variety of levels, from participation in placement reviews to service users having complete control over service delivery. Therefore, depending on the type of participation in question there will usually be an important role to play for social care professionals.

It needs to be recognised that the bulk of service users' participation is on a personal level based on individual situations and requirements. This is understandable and should not be considered negatively. Most people in the UK do not take an active role in developing services and strategic planning.

Social care professionals when working with black and minority ethnic service users need to promote participation in any individual work undertaken. Also there has to be a clear understanding and honesty about circumstances when participation in decision making has to be limited because of the legal and professional obligations of workers such as in childcare proceedings.

Social care, professionals need to support the participation of service users, particularly those from black and minority ethnic communities are a high priority. Not because it is politically correct to do so or government policy demands it, but to develop social care that promotes social inclusion, recognises service users as citizens and enables the agency to provide resources that are based on what service users define as important to them as outcomes.

There is much to be learnt from other social movements about how people who are not members of a particular group (that is, non-disabled people, white people and people who are heterosexual) can be allies and, rightly or wrongly, open doors that may not otherwise be accessible.

Social care professionals can be allies and support service users' participation in a number of ways. The assumption that empowerment and participation requires social care professionals to take a back seat is short-sighted and naïve. Obviously there will be times when black and minority ethnic service users require personal to share experiences, raise concerns, debate issues and agree the what and how of any participation they choose to engage with. Nevertheless, at other times the support of professionals will be required. Begum (1999) gives an example of where the power of the professional was really necessary, yet under the misnomer of empowerment and independence she was told to sort things out herself. 'My social worker recently 'helpfully' told me that I ought to sort out my own disabled parking space as she was supposed to promote independence ... this reminded me of an incident with a GP who told me to write my own medical letter and she would put it on letter headed paper and sign it ... (apparently) she was 'empowering' me. To me it felt as though rather than supporting me as a service user to achieve the outcomes I require, they were discharging their responsibilities and passing the buck to me.... What my GP and social worker don't seem to have grasped in the language of the new world is that it is not only necessary to provide support and resources, but also one has to recognise that sometimes service users spend so much time battling against a brick wall that the professionals need to use their knowledge, power and status to get things moving.'[57]

The concept of partnership working between service users and social care professionals has been popular for a long time and has subsequently become a central plank of participation work. This is something that social care professionals and black and minority ethnic service users could benefit significantly from. However, there needs to an acknowledgement of power differentials and how they may impact on the participation work. Equally, honesty about personal and organisational agendas, decision-making powers, limitations on the work, practical requirements and resources (financial and other) need to be addressed and negotiated upfront.

Caution needs to be exercised to avoid some of the pitfalls of participation work. Trivedi (2002) explains: 'Many (black and minority ethnic service users/survivors) feel that user involvement (based on very sound principles and fought for by the service user movement) has become appropriated by ... professionals who seek to draw users/survivors into their pre-existing professional structures and systems with little regard for whether such systems (usually formal meetings and loads of paperwork) are actually appropriate or relevant to the users with whom they are trying to work. Whilst some users may find these systems useful, others know they are not for them or have learned by bitter experience how disempowering, intimidating and emotionally battering they can be, especially for those who have been most disadvantaged by the system.'[58]

Conclusion

Twenty years ago the notion of service user participation was perceived as something very radical and potentially quite threatening to professionals who had invested a lot of their careers in 'helping' and caring for those who required social care. The growing voice and activism of the service user movement, with a shift in the philosophy and beliefs underpinning social care, meant that service user participation shook the very foundations on which social care was built. Indeed, one senior manager in a social services department said that participation '... would be like letting seal lions run a zoo'.

Fortunately, due largely to the disability and mental health survivors movements, thinking and practice around service user participation has moved on significantly, and it is now much more common place to have service user participation on policies and service delivery in social care, Unfortunately, while participation in the wider service user movement has gone from strength to strength, there has been a gradual decline of black and minority ethnic people with direct experience of requiring or using services being involved in shaping policy and practice to attain the outcomes that they want and need. This decline is surprising, as black and minority ethnic communities in Britain have a strong track record of using personal experience of oppression and discrimination to drive community activism and develop user-controlled services. Moreover, it can be argued that black and minority ethnic people were ahead of the game in terms of working from a participation perspective because those with direct experience of issues such as racism, domestic violence, poor working conditions and so on, were very much in the driving seat when initiating or supporting the process of change.

The reasons why black and minority ethnic service user participation has diminished are varied and complex and this paper identifies some of those reasons, exploring and dispelling some prevailing myths that act as barriers to participation by black and minority ethnic service users. One myth is that participation is happening, albeit through 'substitute service users' such as community 'leaders', black and minority ethnic voluntary sector organisations and black and minority ethnic professionals. The reality is that while community 'leaders', voluntary sector organisations and black and minority ethnic professionals have a role in advocating and representing the interests of black and minority ethnic service users, they do not have direct experience of being social care service users and are themselves not immune to holding stereotypical views of service users and what they need. The message is simple: there can be no substitute for service user participation and short cuts are not the solution.

Additionally, the factors that have helped bring participation to the forefront of social care such as a re-kindling of interest in human rights, citizenship and consumerist and democratic approaches, while important and relevant to black and minority ethnic service users, take on a different meaning when one begins to consider the realities of those communities. A very obvious area of contradiction is that of participation being part of a human rights and citizenship agenda. For instance, the whole concept of human rights and citizenship are brought into question by people's immigration status and history if they are claiming asylum in Britain. Equally, if a black and minority ethnic service user has had considerable difficulty having their basic human needs met, or in receiving support to live independently with their families, then one may easily believe that participation on the basis of democratic and consumerist approaches is a long way from the reality of their lives.

Fortunately, while focusing on the barriers to meaningful participation by black and minority ethnic social care service users, this paper also identifies some current examples of good initiatives. One such initiative, cited in this paper, is a project run by Tasibee, an organisation that started as a Pakistani Muslim women's prayer group. The project worked with Pakistani Muslim women with long-term mental health problems, who, through self-help groups and training, were able to become more assertive and confident.

This paper concludes that there are many positive factors why participation can work for, and with, black and minority ethnic service users. It has drawn on the voices and experiences of black and minority ethnic service users to demonstrate that with the right opportunities, support, resources and the use of a range of participatory approaches there is a commitment from service users to be part of the user involvement agenda and decision-making processes. The paper also warns that to realise this potential it is essential to:

- acknowledge and address immediate needs and personal circumstances
- build trust and allay real fears about getting involved (for example, disabled people from refugee communities)
- have in place the resources and support to enable participation – including social care professionals who can play an all-important and empowering role
- make participation real by having clear parameters of power sharing, relevance, and possible outcomes
- identify ways of supporting individual participation as well as collective/group-based participation
- address the marginalisation of black and minority ethnic service users within mainstream user movements by acknowledging that the service user movement cannot represent black and minority ethnic service users unless 'race' equality issues are both part of mainstream activities and the focus of specific projects
- acknowledge that a change in the participation of black and minority ethnic service users is unlikely to happen in a meaningful way, while the practice of using black and minority ethnic community 'leaders' and black and minority ethnic professionals as a substitute for service user participation continues.

References and note

1. Department of Health (2006) *Our health, our care, our say: A new direction for community services*, Norwich: The Stationery Office, p 13.

2. Department of Health (2006) *Our health, our care, our say: A new direction for community services*, Norwich: The Stationery Office.

3. The phrase 'service user(s)' is used as a way of describing people who are eligible for, receive or require social care resources. It is important to note that not all service users like this phrase or identify themselves in this way. However, for the purposes of writing the term 'service user(s)' is used unless a quotation adopts different terminology, such as 'survivor'.

4. Carr, S. (2004) *Has service user participation made a difference to social care services?*, Position Paper No 3, London: Social Care Institute for Excellence, p 21.

5. Shaping Our Lives et al (2003) *Shaping Our Lives – From outset to outcome: What people think of the social care services they use*, York: York Publishing Services Limited, p 5.

6. Singh, B. (2005) *Improving support for black disabled people: Lessons from community organisations on making change happen*, York: York Publishing Services Limited, p 10.

7. Robson, P., Begum, N. and Locke, M. (2003) *Enabling user-centred user involvement: report of a project to increase user involvement in voluntary organisations*, unpublished, p 3.

8. Wright, P., Turner, C., Clay, D. and Mills, H. (2006) *Participation of children and young people in developing social care*, Practice Guide 06, London: Social Care Institute for Excellence, p 8 (www.scie.org.uk).

9. Arnstein, S.R. (1969) 'A ladder of citizen participation in the USA', *Journal of the American Institute of Planners*, vol 35, no 4, pp 216-224.

10. Wright, P., Turner, C., Clay, D. and Mills, H. (2006) *Participation of children and young people in developing social care*, Practice Guide 06, London: Social Care Institute for Excellence, p 13 (www.scie.org.uk).

11. Robson, P., Begum, N. and Locke, M. (2003) *Developing user involvement: Working towards user-centred practice in voluntary organisations*, Bristol: The Policy Press, p 4.

12. Robson, P., Begum, N. and Locke, M. (2003) *Developing user involvement: Working towards user-centred practice in voluntary organisations*, Bristol: The Policy Press, p 4.

13. Carr, S. (2004) Has service user participation made a difference to social care services?, Position Paper No 3, London: Social Care Institute for Excellence, p vi.

14. Department for Education and Skills (2005) *Youth matters*, London: The Stationery Office.

15 Beresford, P. (2001) 'Service users, social policy and the future of welfare', *Critical Social Policy*, vol 21, no 4, pp 494-512, p 502.

17 Begum, N. (1995) 'Understanding user involvement within a rights based framework', King's Fund Seminar, unpublished.

18 Department of Health (2006) *Our health, our care, our say: A new direction for community services*, Norwich: The Stationery Office.

19 Department for Education and Skills (2005) *Youth matters*, London: The Stationery Office.

20 Carr, S. (2004) *Has service user participation made a difference to social care services?*, Position Paper No 3, London: Social Care Institute for Excellence, pp 21-22.

21 Carr, S. (2004) *Has service user participation made a difference to social care services?*, Position Paper No 3, London: Social Care Institute for Excellence, p 21.

22 Butt, J. (2006) *Are we there yet? Identifying the characteristics of social care organisations that successfully promote diversity'*, Race Equality Discussion Paper 01, London: Social Care Institute for Excellence.

23 www.dti.gov.uk/access/equalitywhitepaper, accessed 11 March 2006.

24 Evans, R. and Banton, M. (2001) *Learning from experience: Involving black disabled people in shaping services*, Warwickshire: Council of Disabled People Warwickshire, pp 2-3.

25 www.reu.org.uk/parenting/htm

26 Downer, J. and Ferns, P. (1998) 'Self-advocacy by black people with learning difficulties', in L. Ward (ed) *Innovations in advocacy and empowerment for people with intellectual disabilities*, Chorley: Lisieux Hall, p 141.

27 Begum, N. (1990) *"... something to be proud of": The lives of Asian disabled people and carers in Waltham Forest*, London: London Borough of Waltham Forest, p 30.

28 Begum, N. (1995) *Beyond samosas and reggae: A guide to developing services for Black disabled people*, London: King's Fund, p 7.

29 Chahal, K. and Ullah, AI. (2004) 'Experiencing ethnicity: discrimination and service provision', *Foundations*, September.

30 Sainsbury Centre for Mental Health (2004) *Breaking the circles of fear: A review of the relationship between mental health services and African and Caribbean communities*, London: Sainsbury Centre for Mental Health, p 8.

31 Begum, N. (2002) 'Black, disabled and still waiting', *Community Care*, 17 October.

32 Ibrahim, F. (2003) 'Prayers, parties and participation', *Mental Health Today*, October, pp 30-32.

33 Begum, N. (2005) '"I'm not asking to live like the queen": the vision of service users (and potential service users) and carers who are seldom heard on the future of social care for adults in England', unpublished, London: Social Care Institute for Excellence, p 3.

34 Begum, N. (2005) '"I'm not asking to live like the queen": the vision of service users (and potential service users) and carers who are seldom heard on the future of social care for adults in England', unpublished, London: Social Care Institute for Excellence, p 3.

35 Department of Health (2005) *Independence, well being and choice: Vision for adult social care in England,* London: The Stationery Office.

36 Begum, N. (2005) '"I'm not asking to live like the queen": the vision of service users (and potential service users) and carers who are seldom heard on the future of social care for adults in England, unpublished, London: Social Care Institute for Excellence, p 117.

37 Ibrahim, F. (2003) 'Prayers, parties and participation', *Mental Health Today*, October, pp 30-32.

38 Begum, N. (1995) *Beyond samosas and reggae: A guide to developing services for Black disabled people*, London: King's Fund, p 12.

39 Butt, J. and O'Neil, A. (2004) *Let's move on: Black and minority ethnic older people's views on research findings,* York: York Publishing Services Limited, p 18.

40 Trivedi, P. (2002) 'Let the tiger roar...', *Mental Health Today*, August, pp 30-33.

41 Trivedi, P. (2002) 'Let the tiger roar...', *Mental Health Today*, August, pp 30-33.

42 Begum, N. (2002) 'Black, disabled and still waiting', *Community Care*, 17 October.

43 Begum, N. (2002) 'Black, disabled and still waiting', *Community Care*, 17 October.

44 Evans, R. and Banton, M. (2001) *Learning from experience: Involving black disabled people in shaping services*, Warwickshire: Council of Disabled People Warwickshire, p 7.

45 Wallcraft, J., Read, J. and Sweeney, A. (2003) *On our own terms*, London: Sainsbury Centre for Mental Health.

46 Sainsbury Centre for Mental Health (2004) *Breaking the circles of fear: A review of the relationship between mental health services and African and Caribbean communities*, London: Sainsbury Centre for Mental Health.

47   Shaping Our Lives et al (2003) *Shaping Our Lives – From outset to outcome: What people think of the social care services they use*, York: York Publishing Services Limited, p 20.

48   Ibrahim, F. (2003) 'Bollywood and beyond', *OpenMind, no* 120, March/April.

49   Morris, S. (1999) in S. Dunn, *Creating accepting communities: Report of the Mind inquiry into social exclusion and mental health problems*, London: Mind (National Association for Mental Health), p 54.

50   Ibrahim, F. (2003) 'Prayers, parties and participation', *Mental Health Today*, October, pp 30-32.

51   Kuyek, J. and Labonte, R. (1995) *Power: Transforming its practices,* Conference report, Prairie Region Health Promotion Centre, University of Saktatchewan/Community Health Promotion Centre, University of Victoria.

52   Singh, B. (2005) *Improving support for black disabled people: Lessons from community organisations on making change happen*, York: York Publishing Services Limited.

53   Singh, B. (2005) *Improving support for black disabled people: Lessons from community organisations on making change happen*, York: York Publishing Services Limited.

54   www.encweb.org.uk

55   www.apda.org.uk

56   www.awaaz.co.uk

57   Begum, N. (1999) 'Walking the talk of empowerment', *Community Care*, 27 October, p 15.

58   Trivedi, P. (2002) 'Let the tiger roar...', *Mental Health Today*, August, pp 30-33.